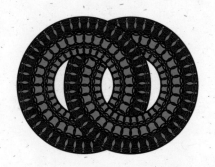

NIGHT SESSIONS

NIGHT SESSIONS

David S. Cho

POEMS

CavanKerry ❖ Press LTD.

Permissions, CavanKerry Press,
6 Horizon Rd., Ft. Lee, NJ 07024.

CavanKerry Press Ltd.
Fort Lee, New Jersey
www.cavankerrypress.org

Library of Congress Cataloging-in-Publication Data

Cho, David S., 1972-
Night sessions / David S. Cho. – 1st ed.
p. cm.
ISBN-13: 978-1-933880-24-2 (alk. paper)
ISBN-10: 1-933880-24-4 (alk. paper)
I. Title.
PS3603.H59N54 2011
811'.6–dc22
2010033072

Cover and interior design by Gregory Smith
First Edition 2011
Printed in the United States of America

NEW VOICES
CavanKerry❦Press

CavanKerry Press is dedicated to springboarding the careers of previously unpublished poets by bringing to print two to three New Voices annually. Manuscripts are selected from open submission; CavanKerry Press does not conduct competitions.

CavanKerry Press is grateful for the support it receives from the New Jersey State Council on the Arts.

CONTENTS

Foreword   xi

I. Family Portraits

Father   5
What is Still   7
The Black Bear   9
Dust   10
The Death of My Cousin   11
The Roller Coaster   13
The Feasting   16
Mourning   18
Grandmother's Watch   19

II. Song of Our Songs

Song of Our Songs   23

III. What the Rain Returns

My Early Linguistic Lesson   37

CONTENTS

Circles   39
Learning to Read   42
The Notebook   44
Friend   46
Simplicity   48
The Bully   49
Water Returning Back to a Well   51
Rain   54
Indian Summer   57

IV. Cheers for Harry Kim

Poems for Harry, #1   61
Poems for Harry, #6   62
Poems for Harry, #7   64
Poems for Harry, #8   66
The Locker Room   68
The Ballerina   71
After the Concert   73

V. Night Sessions

The Shaman   77
Wedding Pictures   79
Night Eyes   80
What My Mother Says When
She Asks Me Why I Write Poems   82
My Bones   83
Driving Home   85
Lake Shore Drive   87
Night Sessions   89

Acknowledgments   91

FOREWORD

For those of us fortunate to have lived awhile, daily, we sift through the turmoil of worldly challenges, tragedy, and take what joy we can in each day. Oh, there are pleasures, but these can be infrequent, clouded by requirements, responsibilities, the rash behavior of a few who frequent the daily bad news, or the many so loudly proclaiming the mundane of life in tweeting frenzy or on facebook pages or youtube videos, and a host of others. William Carlos Williams proclaimed in *Asphodel, that Greeny Flower*, that "it is difficulty to find the daily news in poetry." It is what we do find in good poetry that takes us there again and again, never getting enough of its truth, its revelation of life, one layer at a time. Political scientist, scholar, educator and civil rights activist, Samuel DuBois Cook often said, "there is something about the genuine." That quality of the genuine is what gives poetry its resonance; in David Cho's *Night Sessions*, his verse is a continual blossoming of the genuine. These are well-crafted poems of quiet narratives that reveal a subtle first person persona whose strength is manyfold. Cho makes magic of the mundane. Cho's art is large though quiet with images that linger on affection, sensibility, and taste without being overly sentimental.

First, between the lines telling of a son's awe and awareness of a father's labors, David Cho paints love and the music he learns of man's work, every man, even the poet, from an assembly line. It is this music the son inherits here, the natural tradition of labor and its fruits of many-layered value in these poems that sing such love songs to family without being overly sentimental.

Secondly, there is profound irony in the speaker's war of language, the Korean culture and tongue of parents and family versus the American ways and words of the son. David Cho is at once paying homage to Korean American tradition, Koreans, earnest, hard-working people laden with a desire to belong. Cho appreciates their unique struggle to survive in this foreign land, often unwelcoming, as America fans its flame of flash and expectation, limitation and lack of acceptance. Cho paints a clash of acculturation opposing traditional sensibility within a persona who is observant, respectful with a boyish innocence, engaging us in erudite metaphors, one lovely image one uneasy story at a time.

Then, there is this unimaginable loss, the loosing of the Mother/Father tongue to adopt another, American, one. How does a poet reconcile dreams in his Mother/Father tongue, the language of his heart, in which he does not speak so fluently? This is not just the language of his father, but the true meaning his father understands; and in only a few years, out of necessity, the poet looses his native tongue to Americanization; it's as though the umbilical chord of meaning between the boy and father is cut. David Cho tells us in these poems, which quietly celebrate a life of family love, the discovery of heartfelt connection and question, about Korean family culture and heritage translated into the American experience, painted here for us all to enter and embrace.

The *lagniappe* (Creole for *something extra*) here is the experimental craft, the typographical play and a dance of forms that Cho carves on some pages. Sometimes poets fail at such dangerous attempts; this variety only adds to our pleasure. This designed play and delight are risks Cho takes on the face of some poems on the page without missing a beat, without taxing the reader's journey. There's a narrative poem in columns, and it is no less pleasing or powerful but more so for its virtuosity at play. There's a lyrical listing poem to a bully with concrete images that will bend anyone's memory to childhood. The lyric to "Indian Summer" is ripe with dampness and grass and long hot days. Then, there is the third-person narrative of the charming persona of Mr. Harry Kim; the reader is a fly on the wall watching this Asian boy to man. Then, in "Wedding Pictures," we grin with the uncle learning "only in America do we call each other food." There is no predictable play here, only original painting in words. David Cho's poems are hymns from the heart.

In addition, these poems are quite a tribute from a son to a mother and father, who insisted on a medical doctor, or a Ph.D. in some other acceptable profession, or ascribing to greatness but not a writer. What an apology, what a celebration, what a gift, the verse of David Cho. These poems have hardship and heart; they will touch you deeply, reveal the innocence of a son's desire to please parents; but the persona, this son is courageous enough to carve a poet's life, and a verse worth reading again and again.

Do not be deceived by the simplicity of some of David Cho's verse; there is achievement and power in these *Night Sessions'* poems. Cho's ambition to capture a son's love and admiration between vivid lines of verse makes his achievement memorable, the measure of fine poetry. David Cho's verse sings; it makes a genuine music between son, mother, grandmother, and father, the music of labor, the music, melodic or discordant, between Korean and American sensibility. Here is the epitome of W.E.B. DuBois' twoness, two warring souls, revealed with heart and melody, in metaphors that are never over wrought but fresh and new with each page. The effect of David Cho's verse is not like a trumpet blasting down these two gigantic cultural and linguistic walls, but the soft melodies of a French horn, or a violin, its message infused gently into new territory, what is said and what is not, about family, about two cultures, Korean-American, in one poet we will want to keep.

—*Dr. Mona Lisa Saloy, Author, Folklorist © 2010 NOLA*

To the living memories of

Dong Ku Cho, Young Ja Yoon,
and Martin Cho,
the Cho, Lee, and Yoon clans.

Much love to

my mentors across the states and globe (you know who you are),
and especially,
Sandy, Jonathan, Sarah, and Joanna

NIGHT
SESSIONS

I.
FAMILY PORTRAITS

Father

It is not rain that makes
my father sing a loud
song. I hear a narrow
sound, the thresh of his

sickle, its staccato
making music with his voice.
It draws me near. He calls
this dark marsh field

heaven, the rice to fall,
snow. My father
takes the white
of his palm and lays it

gently on my face.
Two full counts
of callused tenderness,
my eyes sleeping

with the wind. Father says
I am his rice seed,
sprouted to a stalk. The
silence of the field

my only reply. He goes back
to his work, back to make
music, the wooden handle making
his hands hard. He,

the only worker. He
the one worker in this pond.
He in his heaven,
in this field, in his music.

What Is Still

When I was ten, it
was easy to hear
my father. His face

poured over me, a silent
moment of peering
back. What is still

is admiration
for even a father's
whisper. The body

thick
as the hair
stalk was full,

bone gazing
at bone, flesh
peering into its own

begotten. What is still
is memory. In those
days, I was content

with silence, the moments
of my father's face,
the shadow, hovering over me.

Were those pauses prayer—
one overly given
to grieving? What son's

wrong does he grieve? What
man's work makes him cry
rather than rest? What is still

is grief. What was begotten
cannot hold to memory. My father
now leans against

anything straight and rights himself.
His backbone, like his hair,
only a whisper.

The Black Bear

1.

I see through the bars
He does not know
what to do
with his cubs
whose paws
tug and play
his hair
into knots

He would bite
his pups
at the wrist
Rub his short
whiskers
cross their faces
until raw

He is a young bear
that loves
to slumber
Hair like
black smoke
Sleep gristle
in his eyes

2.

When I
was a child
my father
would comb
my hair
to the side
He would
talk about

boot heavy
army days
running hills
Too much coffee
too many cigarettes
aching for food
Hair crew cut

like a bear
He smiled
reminding me
of the Korean myth
We are the mountain
bear's children
restless to go home

3.

Older I
forgot
about the bear
My father
becoming
bald
back stooped
to the ground

Not wanting
to bother
his long stare
I asked how
his health
his hair
his strength was

All Gone
he replied
Asking me to
part his hair
tell him stories
listening quiet now
as if he were the son

Dust

My mouth is dry
because I dream
of apples. Apples,
white and red flesh
wound. Their weight
like full fists of water.
There are apples
in the cupboard,
motionless, their stillness
growing like dust.
I dream of apples,
the dusk growing
black over
the stem and core.
The dried apples leave
a husk like hair
over everything.
Behind the door,
I dream of
apples unwound.
My father would
carefully unrind
the apples,
dry them with salt,
and place them
on my tongue.
The slivers were
the weight of water.
Older now, I slice an apple,
the measure of my father.
The weight of his departure.

DAVID S. CHO

The Death of My Cousin

Once
a buck-
toothed boy
admiring

the
stars, the
constellation,
a gaze in the

circle
of lights.
Comes to
the sill's edge,

slips
out into
the night.
Heaven

opens
a merry-
go-round
with fire.

Black
hair breezes
like smoke
into wind.

NIGHT SESSIONS

My mind
is tinder,
and memory
a fire.

The Roller Coaster

for E. G. Youn 1972-1978

Say to me,
Let's sing a song.

Say to me,
Let's print our hands

on the frosted window glass,
snowflake magnified.

Say to our fathers,
Tell us another story before bed.

The one about the tree, the girl,
the evil stepmother, and the mouse

that saved. Not Cinderella.
The right one—Gonchi Potchi.

Say to me,
Let's go out, laugh again,

leave as young boys into winter's
swirl of snow,

come back
five decades aged,

hair capped white,
as old men.

NIGHT SESSIONS

Say to me,
Let's stay in, in the trash bins,

make like soldiers of war.
I'll wear the white helmet,

be the Buck Rogers,
and you stay in the trash can,

wear the lid, be the robot,
"beedee beedee beedee bee."

You said to me,
Let's make our parents laugh,

dress into traditional "hahmboks"
they wore as kids,

walk stiff-legged
like old village men

from their mountain
hometown in Seoul,

their hands clapping until tears,
then we'll stop.

I want to hear you say,
Let's build a roller coaster

in heaven to know
where to meet someday.

And I want to say,
I'll be there,

when the small car
of the roller ride

clicks to the highest end,
letting go,

curling around
the giant bends

like a fly.
You'll hear me.

The Feasting

Watch my grandmother
fight the sun
with her rag hat
and loose white clothes
that breeze
with the summer wind.

Watch her
plant the seeds,
tiny *dahlgi*,
strawberry hard seeds,
in her left hand—
trembling.

Watch her hoe the ground
with the right hand,
left arm hanging like
a hose, paralyzed
from a stroke
twenty years ago.

Watch my mother's right hand
unrind the *beah*, the pear
down to a carcass,
peeling counter-clockwise
the white freckled skin.
She learned this
from her mother.

I have watched her
do this every dinner
since I was a boy:
lips pressed, eyes narrowed
down to the knife
on skin, she smiles
and leaves a trail,
one curled snake of white flesh.

My mother learned through
hushed supper stories
of her brother fleeing
for the arms of some girl
from the states,
arranged not by custom,
not from Seoul.
Watching her mother cry
until breathless, grandmother
unwrapping the pear whole.

Watch her son
chew the *beah*, listen
to hushed dinner stories retold.
What whispers
sound like laughter
twenty years from the cry.

Mourning

White moon, white lilies
to blossom, the Milky Way
white across the night.
A black bird
repeats
and repeats its caw.
His head cocked,
black eyes not noticing
the frost bitten
morning.
His caw becomes song.
Mother's eyes tilt,
drinking in the early morning light.
She detects nothing,
but a bird's
curt caw.
This posits a thought:
I've more sadness than you,
more than can be sung.

Grandmother's Watch

I have seen my brother's back
become one high back-
packed yard of books.
Not one book from class,

coming home,
he'd carry them all.
He would make like a mother.
Mothers we've seen

in photographs,
carrying their babies
in rags at their back,
like bundles of laundry

to wash by hand,
carrying the world
on their hips.
This is no myth.

My grandmother,
paralyzed by a stroke,
made her way to our yard,
and hoed it, planting onions:

white bulbs and green tubes
we ate for a year with soup, with stew,
with rice. These women weren't as short
as rice stalks, but close,

and had I never teased them
I might be tall as a tree
and not stout as a stump,
carrying my books

like Atlas's world, its ball
chained to my shoulders,
short legs, bowlegged knees
pumping up and down

as I walk home
behind my brother from school.
During dinner and homework after,
our legs keep pumping like a twitch.

We try not to bite our nails raw
like the hands of old widows
with work to do.
They might be watching.

II.
SONG OF OUR SONGS

Song of Our Songs

1

I am an insomniac.
I write at night in my kitchen.
I write only on dead winter nights, where of all things in Indiana,
    tonight, it rains.

What to do on these cold winter nights, when rain comes down
    hard as sleet.
What to do with rain that freezes the windows, grid through a
    screen.
What to do with the sound of rain like the furnace air coming
    through the vent.

2

I would die to write a poem
to my father

in his tongue.
Korean.

The smooth roll
of syllables and words

which held me
captive as a baby,

spoken by my father, mother,
and their mothers, brothers, and sisters,

the tree of life,
that lineage

written ages ago on a scroll
and shown to me:

"You are a Punyang Cho
honored class of Korea,

a Yangban. You are next,
what will you do?

Oh deu gae hal guh yah?
How will you make us proud?"

This hypnotic
tongue

I forgot
at age seven

when my father left
to sweep steel factory floors,

and mother would leave for Sears
bringing back small cardboard boxes

of defective Hans Solos
Luke Skywalkers, action figures

she detected on the assembly line,
saving enough money

to move
to the suburbs of Chicago.

On that cold winter day,
I was told to learn English,

to utter the dim nave
of a language they once learned.

My mind turned
like uneven gears in a clock:

how to go from,
Ahn young hee ha sae yo,

"Hello, how are you," a phrase
intoned to honor,

head bowed,
eyes never level

with an elder;
to this white lady teacher

smiling at me in the eyes, saying,
"Hey you, hi yuh doin?"

The Korean language now
comes to me in pieces:

Pan gap seub ni dah,
"Nice to meet you,"

Pae gu pa dah,
"I am hungry,"

Ahn yong hee ga sae yo,
"Good-bye, you are leaving."

It is the only language
my heart knows,

but my tongue
so many times, refuses.

3

How to write
a poem

in a native tongue,
a tongue

conceived
an ocean away

and brought here
like a letter

shipped in a boat
silent as a ship

slipping away
in the waves

postmarked, stamped,
and delivered by my father.

I would die
to put this in a letter,

in a tongue
my father could read.

Place it in his casket,
like flowers,

if it took that long,
all my life.

4

I exaggerate.

There was no ship, there was no boat.

I exaggerate again.

There was me and mother on a plane.

I was in her womb.

S.S. Placenta.

5

Today I kiss my wife
remembering to say, *gandah*,

or "I am leaving," an intoned phrase—
half fact and supplication—

as if she could say
"No, stay home with me today,

do not leave for work
in the early morning light"

as I did as a child,
fearing never to see my mother again.

Gandah. She would quietly say,
as if to not disturb my sleep,

leaving me with only a kiss
to remember.

6

Memory, you always have me groping for my past.
Memory, it's loss—
Memory, you betray me like the kiss of Judas.

Memory, I kiss you on the cheek and write.

7

I won't forget.
I once visited Korea. I've been there twice since.
I rode a plane the first time,

And saw hundreds of palm trees, half sized, like Koreans
        cramming into lines,
shoving signs in my face, *Sung Yoon, Yoon Shik Ah, Yi Sung Min,*
        I remained silent, waiting for a voice like my father's, stern,
        last name first—

Joh Sung Woo?

        And saw an old man, fully my father—thin waisted, tight
        lipped, grey faded suit, with sharp pointed, black horned
        rims—some thirty years before the advent of *Mad Men.*

"Older father?" *Geun Ah Buh Jee?*

Then I dreamt my father, his brother, their father at a Seoul tavern.
    "How rich we were until grandfather lost his election," they
    said—then the war—then mother sewing clothes out of war
    surplus bags.

The tongue of my fathers turned in a wheel, with no stop of flow—

I was dreaming in Korean.

I was so proud. I called my parents. They were proud.

Going home, I looked down at the squatty trees, the plane
    ascending into clouds, sending me away, where by black
    hair, pale skin, kim-chi eating, stubby body—

I belonged.

8

I am here.
I am at church past midnight.

Darkness peering in the windows,
cold December air reaching through,

hissed warm by the pipe
heaters, clanking like a boiler

of a train to begin.
The sound of snow

falling on the roof.
The silence.

Creaking wood
that sounds like angels

on the pews around me,
or perhaps some demon ghosts

sit, creaking the wood,
the noise,

the thought—
I begin to pray.

9

I was taught to pray:
bottom on heel,
toes and knees on the ground,
arms crossed or hands pointed upwards.

We were taught to pray,
all legs and arms bent straight and diagonal,
curled up like a letter "z,"
praying to Jesus, but we looked like Buddha.

We prayed silently as the rock Buddha statues
I had seen as a boy.
When I was a teen,
someone began to cry.

We all looked and cried the same. Why not?
We prayed for her, we prayed for her
desperate need, became desperate in our prayers.
We prayed as if someone were to die.

We prayed like a stone, its black core
aged over time, heat and pressure,
what had long ago seeped
from its tiny fissures—

hardened into a shell.
This was our silence, our meditation.
Somedays now, I feel like that stone—quiet,
waiting to cry out.

10

If you don't believe me, ask my friends
John, Steve, Mike, or Dale.

Take a boy who was given away by his mother,
his father a sailor, or a rich man with mistresses,

or a U.S. Vet who suddenly departed for home.
Take that boy, place him with good German-American

or Anything-American parents. Let him grow.
Let him grow his parents' way.

Let him grow to college hardly knowing any Koreans
except for what he sees on TV or in newspapers.

Let him go to those Korean dry cleaners, beauty supply stores,
doctor offices or restaurants,

and let him taste a jar of kim-chi,
fermented rice cabbage in red pepper juice.

Give him some time to get over the smell,
as if something had died in the container.

He'll go hungry for that—
hot juiced, dry cabbage,

or have tabasco sauce with his eggs, steak, or rice.
He'll put a jar of it in his fridge.

That is the way with us in prayer.
All pickled up,

far from home
and needing some spice.

11

If you still don't believe me, hear my mother sing hymns, psalms,
     old folk songs; narrow eyes into round saucers, throat
     opening, vibrating, songs that cut through the air; first my
     mother, then her sister, then the baritone of my father.

My friends and I would play sing, pluck our throats, try to sing
     vibrato too.

We'd sleep when they prayed, running away with the last Amens,

Wanting to play kickball, football—anything with a ball.

Young, too young for their revival.

People praying to the ching-ching tempo of the guitar string,
     praying like wolves in a pack,

praying as if the moon were full,
praying to be the donkey Jesus rode into Jerusalem,
people praying, praising Him, like the palms laid down at this
    arrival,
bodies swaying to the music, like wind-blown reeds.

Twenty years old, still with my friends, I laughed at the cacophony
    of cries.

Then the light clicked on in the room of darkness.

Sitting in the balcony, I looked down.

I knew this father they cried to.

A father who told us what to do.
A father who had much to say.
A father who was silent.
A father who wanted us home.
A father who left his home.

A father who killed himself to show his love.

The clothes I wore—bought by my father.
The language I longed for—spoken by my father.
The half smile of joy I hid—modeled after my father.
What life I was to live—written into my book-sized head, written
    by my father.

God rested on the seventh day, and listening to my father's
    Sunday morning breathing, deep underwater breathing, I
    understood: so does my father.

12

Tonight I'll go visit my father's grave,
a place in suburban Chicago he's bought already.

I'll visit the grassy spot, undug, and the plot for my mother there
     too,
and say, *Anh young hee ga sae yo,* "Good-bye, you are leaving,"
bow two and half times, as I was instructed as a boy.

My father isn't near passing away, but I'll do it anyway,
hoping he will hear me across the expanse of sky,
blue as a dark bruise after night rain.

I'll read this in Korean and leave the poem by the gravestone-to-be.

I'll try my best.

May they tuck it away in some chest they'll carry to the grave.

May that bring him comfort as he sleeps.
May that bring sweet memories of me in my mother's dreams.

III.
WHAT THE RAIN RETURNS

My Early Linguistic Lesson

Because I was lonely,
moving to the white house
and sidewalked

suburbs of Chicago,
and needing
to get out

and make some friends,
I went to the park, where
they would BMX jump

on a hill, all evening long
until it grew too dark for
even the buzzing bulb lights.

Invariably, one would say
"fuck you" and I would blink
and not understand—

was it "You,
fuck you-
rself"

or "I
will fuck
you."

I was still a boy
who believed that babies
came from my mother's stomach.

NIGHT SESSIONS

And in either case—
my interpretation
or their proposition—I preferred neither

and would say, "No."
They would laugh,
so mouth open wide,

their teeth shone
yellow like the bulbs, and white
as the cement and stars that night.

Circles

I look in the rear
view mirror to
the growing hole
in my head. At ten,
I would walk, alone,
to the playground
trying to understand
kickball, baseball,
football, see kids shrieking
at one another, tiny
men at war. They spoke
too fast for me. I
would wander, wondering
from what I saw on TV,
why the Lone Ranger
had Tonto; and King David,
Jonathan; Batman
and Robin, and I
had no one. I would
try to join them,
sprinting hard to first, kids
would tease me, asking
if I knew where I
was going. I did not.
I wandered around
the neighborhood, north
and south, veering east,
and west, not knowing
the difference. I
walked until day

grew dusk, wide eyes
open, giving way
to sleep. My tired head
a compass, twirling
from pole round to
the other pole. This is
where the hole began.
Awake, alone, I
wandered around
my school years
with a compass
in my hand,
wondering if there
were needles instead
twirling in my head,
building to building,
school to home.
I drive now, years
older, wiser, my
hole now wider,
and peer at the sky.
The birds and what
they leave behind, like
the rain, could fall in—
not good for my hole.
These rainy days, I
wonder if a woman
could learn to love me,
if our kids would
inherit this hole,
and if my sons
would be ashamed—combing
their hair over, or
covering their heads

with a hat—cursing
this hole. Rainy days
like these, they core me.
Not knowing whether
to turn right or left,
not knowing when
the hole began,
then I realize—
I'm in my old
neighborhood, at the park,
and have driven a
whole life's circle.

Learning To Read

I see a boy through the gaps
made by piling leaves on leaves
like stone on stone.

His fort is fragile as the boy's hand
waving wildly in that wind,
catching more leaves, stone

for the fort, leaf for his dream
of hiding himself
until dusk grows dark,

scribbling words from books,
a notebook of dissimilar things,
to feed his father at dinner:

how to say *clothesline,*
how to use the word
ferocious in a sentence, what
the Korean equivalent of *desire* might be.

"Delicious," father, say it—
cut your tongue on the top teeth for "l,"
let "r" hang free in the middle cave of your mouth.

The young boy does a difficult thing—
he sits and reads,
pondering to posit an answer.

The winds pry, trees sheave, the leaves
become red dirt in his palm—the sky
black-blue as a bruise—silent as trees.

The Notebook

It is not that he meant
to kiss me, that his lips
press into a tight zero.

No, Father,
the tongue cuts "l" into the top teeth
and "r" makes you pucker.

Was it an interrogation
where a man stands with a notebook,
zeroing in on the words

of his son's lips? Or
was it a translation, his
tongue tied, shocked

by this English speaking boy—
who by pale complexion, mop hair,
and same small nose, could not utter

a full phrase of the father's tongue?
No, Father, "ascribe" is to attribute something,
to someone, a motive, or quality, I said.

And "describe" is what one says
about that person. And yes, Father,
"a scribe" is the one who will

write all this down, like Mr. Webster.
To this, my father proudly *described*
how his first son would *ascribe* to

greatness, like King David,
perhaps as a doctor though. And
like *a scribe*, he would write down

this prophecy—
to see it so. I was ten,
notebook in hand.

Friend

in memory of Khoi Nguyen, 1972-1991

I'll tell you a story.

If you listen carefully,
you can hear the cries of this jungle.

The tiger longing for some place, some-
where dry to sleep. The angry growling, he can

not find a lot bare
and sparse. Restless tiger instead lies in the tall grass.

I'll begin again.

My friend lay under a tree. I dreamt that his thick hair
grew wild,

that his hair draped long over his body. That his face creased
in age. I dreamt

that between his lips, I placed a rose. Red. His hot breath
smelled like flower fumes,

and its thorns grew wild.

Here is the point.

We are in a rice paddy. The thick grain grass covers our legs. The
    water bowlegs our walk.

The clouds streak by, the sky stained a moon-red. It scares my
     breath

to sprint in bursts, and he slumps over.

Here's what happened:

My Vietnamese friend, at age nineteen. Gone to have some rest.

Simplicity

My brother asked me what simplicity was.

So we boarded a plane and flew to Korea, but the dinner choices
were too confusing.
We boarded a fishing boat and came back to the states, but the
time zones left us a day behind and sick from its difference.
We rode a BMW, closed its windows, played loud music, rode the
Eisenhower highway,
never heard the police following until we got a ticket.
We walked, but we bickered over directions in the streets of
Chicago.
We stopped in a café, but choosing coffee was like being back
overseas, speaking a foreign tongue.
We called our mother but she asked us what we were bickering
about.
We asked a professor and were told to read Nietzsche.
We read Nietzsche and were filled with rage. *God is dead? How
could this be?*
We filled our rage by pumping fire hydrant water over each other.
We peed in the Chicago River because of all the water we drank.
We lay out on the beach to dry, but our shoes filled with sand.
We went barefoot into the lake, swam like young kids worried
about piranhas.
We fished for them until the sun made us lobsters of skin.
We filleted what we fished.
We fried the fillet.
We napped until the sun came down,
Until half the sun floated, its red crown folding into the black-blue
lake horizon

The Bully

The boy whose father bought him a BMX bike, the first on our block;
The boy whose father bought him *Playboy* and *Penthouse*;
The boy whose eyes looked like two whole saucers;
The boy whose hair looked straight as the teeth comb;
The boy whose mother spit to shine his hair;
The boy whose brother was the first beatnik on our block and
      smoked;
The boy whose brother became my cousin's friend;
The boy whose brother was the model I was instructed by my
      mom to never become;
The boy whose brother dropped out of school;
The boy whose fists pummeled my right eye into a swollen "O,"
      five times;
The boy whose muscles took us two years to match up;
The boy, who was first to grow pubic hair—and much more;
The boy who could first throw a pocket knife into the dirt, blade first;
The boy who refused to say, "WE will BE LOyal Scouts;"
The boy who swore so profusely, was kicked out, and had to give
      back his "WEBELOS" patch;
Which is to say, the boy said, "Go blow," to the den mother;
The boy who swore to ridicule my quarter saucer black eyes, was,
The boy whose father always wore a blue mechanic jumpsuit
      with his name—"*Tony*"—in red-stitch cursive, on his left;
The boy whose father punished him, stick-to-hide, cussing in front
      of us;
The boy whose mother punished him for learning to cuss, "Where
      would he learn that?";
The boy whose father did not like to leave or be bothered from
      his garage;
The boy whose father made apple cider jugs swell with his own
      urine wine;

The boy whose name was hard as his fists—"Toni Wudi;"
The boy whose "picks" in basketball cleared the floor;
The boy whose blocks for me in high school football were as wide
    as the Red Sea
and I was the Asian American Moses running the ball;
The boy, I had faith in him like a mustard seed:
The boy whose hits leveled low the Glen Ellyn Hilltoppers;
The boys whose jersey number was 99, and liked it, the
    cheerleaders loved it;
The boy, he loved the cheerleaders chanting it, chanting it;
The boy who gave me rides home in his Ford pick up;
The boy, he placed his jock on the antenna, the one our gym
    teacher checked for, people staring at the "burn out" and
    "Oriental," like we were Butch Cassidy and the Sundance
    Kid, the reincarnated colors of a Twinkie;

The boy, he showed me how to salute these people, middle finger
    out—*just to show everyone their IQ*—flashing that freckled
    ear-to-Toni-Wudi-ear smile.

Water Returning Back to a Well
for Sung Man Choi 1972-1997

1

It is raining today.
You can hear the water

coming down
like the furnace air

up through
a grilled vent.

The rain is water
returning back

to a well
we drink from.

2

Rain is what keeps us,
kept us, from turning

into dust, like the dust
kicked in our mouths,

chest heaving
from running on the asphalt

courts,
heaving the basketball.

Friend,
how easily

hope gave to gladness
when the ball,

a red moon,
punctured the night,

a hole through the flat line
of a rim.

We were dehydrated,
returning for water,

rubber legs
and exam worries

bringing us home.
Water is what kept us,

water drunk cool
down our throats.

Water returning back
to its own well.

3.

Odd days like these
bring tornado warnings:
bleeps across the TV screen
and low-voiced

warnings on the radio.
The air full and heavy,
shaking the trees empty
as beggars, wind whistling

sharply through the window,
small sacs of air driving
the whirlwind, but rain
hardly hitting the ground.

Humid eddies collect
and collect, the wind
driving the rain
through the brick wall

like straw I once heard
went through
a barn's wood
straight as a nail.

Rain

for Stephen Haruch

I hear many voices, or
one voice
repeating

until nothing else
remains, and I call you by one
name,

though you answer
to another.
I hear

one sound.
The wet grass
contains

no rain, only
water. The act of falling
given form. The shaken air,

the branches nodding,
two leaves
joined together,

turning over
each other
heavy with rain,

which is not
weight
but momentum,

they can tell, retell
each other
every autumn.

I hold a shell
to my ear.
What I hear

is not the ocean,
but rain,
which is a story

the ocean tells,
told, and retold.
Return, it says.

I too
have a story
which I tell,

have told,
and know it retold
by the rain

that falls
in a place where you
were born

and left since,
where I have
only my uncles, aunts, and cousins.

What remains
between us
is water,

which has no face.
Where you once lived
I will go

to the only sound
we know,
which is not rain,

but what the rain returns.

Indian Summer

These are the days stretched long. The weeks
when darkness sets, then the rain, the falling leaves,
frost, the early morning light. These are the days
when light breaks, holding the night, and turning
leaves red. These are the long days, the ladybugs
making their final turn, flurry of red wings,
scissoring in procession upwards. Let not a young child
bottle their journey; let their migration up trees,
up wind be longer. Let not the children's games
be interrupted. Their shallow pantings: bat, ball,
tag: let their nervous joy be longer.
The leaves settle on the grass, red peat
makes the ground damp. The ripe smell of cut
grass and fallen leaves. Its damp sweet weight
falls on ponds; fish greet the ripeness, rise,
their lips open. The fishermen are happy.
Let the weight linger longer. Windows open,
curtains spill out from the house.
Let these summers be gloried; and these red peat days,
the glory we long for.

IV.
CHEERS FOR HARRY KIM

Poems for Harry, #1

Harry Kim awakens,
hears what might be the cooing
of birds in the early morning half light
yet dark, runs down the hallway

to see his father kneeled
before a chair as a pastor would
before an altar or pew.
He is praying, Harry discovers,

in a tongue that seems to come
from the heavens, or at least
the rafter of pigeons above.
And in silent reverence

which equals love for his father,
Harry imitates that strange roll
and garble of unintelligibles
in his mind and later through

his own lips. He practices them,
imagining their original meaning,
becoming a meditation of sorts,
a young child whose brows knit

together in a furrow, closing out
time, listening to the curtains unfold,
smelling the dust gathering
in rays through the open window slits.

Poems for Harry, #6

Harry never saw his parents
hold hands, let alone

kiss, as sometimes the parents
of the neighborhood kids would

coming home before dinner.
But Harry would see his parents

sitting inches away
from another.

Mrs. Kim would roll sesame-oiled rice,
spinach, yellow pickled radish, and long

pieces of meat into a bamboo mat,
pressing the roll tight.

Mr. Kim would watch,
eyes half opened, as if to sleep,

how he loved to see the rolls sliced vertically,
the white, yellow and black slivers separating.

Cut clean through the core, precise
as the rhythm of her "Amens"

uttered between the pauses
of her pastor and husband's prayer.

The slices, black
as a lacquer plate

hanging on their wall:
Two silver men eating

from a pearl potted rice,
the moon shining like a nickel,

savored in the mouth
of a man who would work all night,

come home, watch his wife,
take the thin yellow-snake,

mud, teeth, and long grass
colored strips and shards,

and roll them together again,
like a potter.

Poems for Harry, #7

To know what happiness is
go to the church that Mr. Kim
labored over, Lazarus-like: an old school,

bought with the mortgage on his house,
repaired with his own hands, and begun
with only a congregation of three—pastor,

wife and child. Go to the Busse Woods picnic
they have every year, when all the Koreans come out
promising to attend every week after this.

Watch them relax their tired legs on the straw mats,
fan themselves from the heat of the summer,
refreshed by the smell of rice, slender long fish,

gongchi, on the grill, marinated meat and *kim chi* for lunch.
See the people gather to brag about their children—
their honor rolls, the new piano and violin

prodigies of the century. They'll gorge on the gossip,
fill their bellies, take a nap, then the games begin.
One will pull out a soccer ball, and the men

become boys, pushing one another to get to the ball,
tuck in their guts, stretch out their stubby legs,
and run as if the family's honor

like some prize in heaven were waiting,
running like the days they served in the army,
three years given for the love of their country,

never knowing how difficult it would be to work
as an immigrant in the U.S.; where in the 70s,
the sting of Nam and Pearl Harbor

brought them hard looks from their bosses
and fellow workers. For three hours, they forget all this,
content to know one another, hear their children

and wives laugh, letting the sun lobster their skin,
for as long as it still remains day.

Poems for Harry, #8

after Philip Levine

To know what work is,
watch Harry, a young boy,

burn his thumb on the pot of water,
checking if it has boiled

enough to place a few beef franks in it.
Boil them red, broth foaming from the fat

and long beef sacks. Watch Harry
put the franks and the yellowed beef-fat soup

into his father's Thermos, pack a smaller Thermos of coffee,
and a bag of rice, chanting to go with his father.

Help him clean the spit, gum and mud of the kids he played
with at school, wash the windows clean, and make

porcelain white-clear
what Harry's friends made black with their bowels and bladders.

Watch Harry leave for school
as his father comes in from third shift,

goes to his study, prays for a while, letting his hands
straighten from the mop's hold, his hair dry out

from the sweat and ammonia, his mind cleaning out, praying
to his God for sweet rest, strength for the next night,

laying alms, supplicating that the few dollars, *kim chi*,
rice and *pulogogi* would fall like manna,

grow like loaves and fishes.
See his fingers callous over the years,

turning dark from lack of oxygen.
See him stay up to study and prepare for the next

Sunday's message.
Watch Harry's eyes gleam when his father,

bagged eyes and all,
tells Harry that he drank down the food,

rice, meat, soup and all—it was good—
for it was made by his only son,

and that Harry must study hard,
prepare for the unexpected turn in life,

work hard as his father,
for, before the Lord,

that is what work is.

The Locker Room

1

It is a secret thing, though it does not seem a secret
to Harry. He and other Asian boys
he meets do not do like other boys do

in the locker room. Some men, with their
washboard bodies, walk around naked
as the Greek David, and as long and full

in places where no leaf could cover.
Others have bellies that sag,
with penises that sag all the more

like overripe fruit on a tree, whose
skin is rotting off, everything out like laundry
to dry, but far be it for the boys to stare,

though they do in silence. There are men
as small as twin pods hanging from a leaf,
and others full as a curved plantain.

But a man's fortune or misfortune does not help them:
Should the Asian boys walk around, bravado-like, as the others?
What if they are not macho enough in size

to cavalier their parts that so many bragged of,
jokes, where most boys laughed, but Harry
and the other boys, Asian, blinked to understand,

listened in silence, imitated, and joined
in the laughs of the many. So here they stand
in a high school locker room, sliding

their shorts off, wondering, if, how,
and how long to shower naked as the others
washing their privates with soap,

lathering themselves clean,
the white foam sliding off their skin
like semen.

2

In Korea, Harry recalls, all men: boys,
young men, and the elderly, would go to a public
bathhouse, sit in the steamed

water, then in the ice cold water;
after a day of doing both,
all were pruned loose, relaxed, and small,

wet buddhas sitting in meditation. But in America,
Harry's friend, Shin Huk, thinks the shower etiquette
the same, and while showering, lets loose

his bladder, the yellow liquid spilling on the floor.
But this is not the Far East. Before the urine
washes away the soap and water, swirling

into the drainpipe, the boys squealing in horrified delight,
pointing to Shin, "Shit, why'd you do that?"
"Shin, shit—it's ok—go ahead!" as if he were filthy,

a pig, leaving his entrails out for all to see, perhaps later,
eating from his own excrement. Harry stays silent,
wishing it were over.

He wets a towel, wipes himself off,
sliding on his shorts, calling it a day,
heading home quickly,

the biting laughter spreading
like the steam, sliding through the narrow
cracks of the door, opening, shutting,

shutting and opening.

The Ballerina

The girl was dressed in tights,
everything she wore in fact was tight.
Tight enough that her breasts seemed

swollen under the press
of the gown, her hair kept
in a bun, stretching her face

thin, the heavy powder
making her face pale
as the dead.

Harry watched in fascination
every leap, curve, and dance
that came alive

with the music
and changing colors
behind her.

Standing on her toes,
leaping from them, pirouetting,
her small dress creating circles

in the dark. She brought whispers,
from the audience, Harry too.
There Harry found himself

swept in her moves,
her pale face, emotionless. He imagined
her mind like an engine, whirring

NIGHT SESSIONS

a few steps ahead,
a mind blanking out
the next day's criticism

or this day's applause, a mind
delivering moves to the next
run of strings or boom

of the low drums,
a mind that pictured
the moves of the teacher

before her.
There in the front row
where people sat silent,

Harry pitied the ballerina
for such a doomed life
of pleasing others,

yet found himself oddly
weeping into the open circle
of his sleeve,

the people clucking
like hens
at this commotion.

DAVID S. CHO

After the Concert

Harry went home that night,
turned on the same adagio of strings
he had heard earlier,

the music speaking to him
words that were not there,
just as Harry's memory

of his father was there
but faded, knowing his father
would be pleased with his

growing love
for the run and
blend of violin.

The ballerina,
her pale outline going round
as the record

on the stereo turned,
a moment
where to Harry

words became
a dark ink
seeping into

the blank page,
a prayer of sorts,
a meditation, occasion

to write down.
But this, Harry knew,
would displease his father,

a word wasted
in something that could have been
instead a night of cold labor,

silence,
and a morning given in words
of prayer.

V.
NIGHT SESSIONS

The Shaman

After watching hours of TV—
Daisy in her short cut-off jeans,
and Daisy, the dandelion eating

dog—mindlessly drawn by
what I see, but is not
really what's there in the box,

I look through the window.
And there's a young man in my parking lot
whom I've seen at the bookstore

yelling "Canadian Bacon" as if he were hungry,
screaming with unusual delight, people staring.
I turned away. This Chinese boy,

maybe twenty years of age, with my cousin's crew cut hair—
the cousin who held out a handful of berries
from my lawn bush, me thinking *I know they're poisonous*

as he swallowed them down whole—this cousin
I loved like my brother. His slim jawed face
with square black frames, bottle thick lenses
both their faces hid behind.

I've seen this stranger at the church picnic,
where hundreds of Koreans
meet for rice, marinated meat, fish on the grill,

after we've sung our hymns and last *Amens*,
he ran through the fields, hands raised
as if finishing a marathon,

all by himself. No one saw this but me.
And now, it's promising to rain—
you can hear it in the thunder,

and he is standing above this red Chevette
that has not started for weeks,
his hands raised above his head

like a shaman, trying to bring the car
back to life. I try to go out there,
share an umbrella. He walks away,

head tilted, body twitching forward.
It begins to rain and I think,
that should be me.

Wedding Pictures

The photographer asks my fiancee to sit in my lap.
We do not oblige, knowing my uncle who grins
every time he hears a man call his wife "honey,"
thinking *only in America do we call each other food,*
only here do we keep our dogs inside like babies
and treat them like sons with choice meats from the table.
        In Old Korea, we would do otherwise.
I think of Sandy's parents, married by a city official,
only parents at their weddings, twenty minutes
to wed—no altar kiss. Come to think of it—no late night
phone calls in all these weeks before, no coffee talks,
just parental arrangement. Sandy's father
took a late night walk once, peeking over a wall.
      I see the pictures of my parents,
their wedding, my father's black hair slicked to the right,
my mother's hair in a bun. He stands rigid
as a tree, my mother sits to his right, upright
in a chair, their fingers inches apart, half smiling,
half not.

Night Eyes

My mother's hair is silver
as the moon's reflection
off the el-train in Chicago

that she rode on nights
working the third shift.
She would come back a ghost

from the late hours,
eyes squinting for sleep. I remember this.
Her hair was black as ink

until you two boys were born,
my father tells me with love, rubbing
black dye into her hair with a brush.

This I did not know: one night
she came home staggering with a prescription
in her right hand, saying,

Never worry again
about the flower in our window
blossoming and bearing its own likeness every year.

Today she tells me this:
Had I known we would do so well,
you would have more siblings.

I drove back to school that night
traveling through Chicago,
a train passing overhead—

I heard its rattling, saw it scatter
gravel and leaves, the red tail lights
like eyes in the night, fading and gone.

What My Mother Says When She Asks Me Why I Write Poems

When the birds rise,
circling up the tailwind,
will you be like one—

    tethered to a line,
    behind, spinning
    with few words,

face so heavy to lift,
your silence
riveting the ground?

My Bones

When the butterflies are gone,
  someone give my son my
bones in a brown bag.
  Let him open the bag,
see the collarbone
  his father broke while diving
to catch a football. Give him
  the ligament, hard as a hose,
torn while trying to make
  a block. Barely able
to lift his arm and stand,
  he walked to his car,
paid three tolls, drove home
  wondering how much
one could suffer
  for manhood and a ball.
Let my son see
  the right hand bones
of his father. Hand
  that loved his wife's face:
wide eyes, hair—a crown
  of blackness, brows
thin as match sticks, for such
  tiny loveliness, he'd use
two hands and have
  no regrets. Two hands—
are they not better than one?
  Let my son see his father's
broken right hand, flat palm
  that collected my mother's hand

and her tears, lamenting
  it would never be the hand
of a surgeon or the fingers
  of a pianist. One night I awoke
as she tried to curve back
  my hand, and in her sorrow
I promised to curl my hand
  around a pencil, write her poems.
Someone give my son
  that bag, let him play
with my bones: a ligament to bend
  when he's bored. Give him that bag
to play with on a quiet day,
  let him build back
the bones of his father,
  I'd rather be with him
this way, to haunt him—
  but letting him stand up
to the old man, fearing him a bit.

Driving Home

I want to be driving
across a bridge, pass
the factory chimneys
burning sulfur, a night light
to this industrial town—Gary, Indiana.
I want to drive past
the bead-sweat glimmer of factory men,
toward Chicago church crosses
high as the highway. Pass
the old cement school yard
where I learned kickball,
kids smoking in the sewer—
its graffiti walled tunnels.

I want to keep driving, somehow
drive to the town of my father's birth,
see his teenage face, body made lean
and rough by the rugby scrums
and running up hills
with his brother with a barrel.
One would push the barrel up
and follow the other
lying inside, head out,
riding down like a wheel.
Both crying in joy, panting for air.

Drive me to those Seoul mountains,
place of my buried lineage.
Bury me beside my thirteenth
father before me, who trying to be
like his grandfather-become-governor,

ran from the farm, made money in banking,
lost as mayor, and returned home
as the farmer's champion
almost made big. Speak to me
of my father—who by army commission
ran rugby field laps rather
than basic training.

I hear people say
how his swollen lips,
black eyes, nose and brows
fixed to a T, are mine.
I would run until my feet were flat,
lungs spent, hills worn to the ground.
Something in me wanting to die,
to hear what was once said
of my father, become me.

Lake Shore Drive

Here on Lake Shore Drive
you can eat curry, buffet-style,
exit on Devon, no meat for $2.95,
see the pawn shops and pink elephant signs;

and on Belmont, see cultural balance at its finest,
an Oyver Roman Gift Shop proclaiming,
tenemos telofonicas tarjetas para vender,
a young Korean boy staring at "Michael,"

prodigious tongue exposed, like an offensive flasher,
posterizing a Pacer, asking for "Classic Air Jordans,"
not the sneaker-white ones—the old school ones—
red as the Bulls' head, black as the two-capped nostrils
emitting smoke, a Sloan and Van Lier-like,

mean and gritty, defensive trap.
Go to Lawrence, hear the karaoke bass,
eat the seasoned fried legs of chicken,
meat dumplings, and buy a pizza: sausage,
cheese, and fermented rice cabbage—
kim chi—for spice on top.

To know happiness, go to Hyde Park
in the summer, where Latinos lay down their shirts,
let their long hair and Spanglish flow,
playing soccer for dinner.

To know sadness, visit Wrigley Field,
and be me for one day in just this:
ballpark of green ivy, nectar of Bud-
weiser, don't tell anyone—I love the Cubs.
Why not? God blessed the suffering of Job.
God bless the heart of Harry Caray.

To know sorrow, stand by me
at a Dempster St. funeral where a mother
of my friend stops breathing
from her sobbing,

becomes a Korean coiled "s,"
all knees and shoulders heaving
on the ground as her
son's casket is lowered.

We are singing a hymn—
for I know my redeemer lives
and I will stand
with him on that day.

She wants
to follow him to the grave, but
her husband holds her back.

All around us, the rain has stopped,
leaves turn over in the wind.
The hymn is not yet over.

Night Sessions

Why my Korean brothers do not talk
in class, I do not know. They
wait like children around
a piñata, waiting to strike
the teacher's question,
make the world turn
with silencing answers of God.
Late night talks of the eternal
make them sleepy headed for class,
miss the assignments, pull all night sessions
to try and score perfectly, knowing
it is too late, make them work
all the harder, their faces furrowed
the color of ash.

If you don't believe me,
watch them play basketball
at midnight. Stout Korean bodies
flying, making their own
pale light, making the ball rise
like a red moon, a prayer
thrown up to God, leaving books
for exams stacked high behind
in faith, leaving the silence
of parents locked in stores,
shoulders hunched, bowlegged,
exhausted, wondering whether
their children knew—*all this was done for you*—.

NIGHT SESSIONS

How they love this game until dawn,
dark bodies, the soot of asphalt,
thud into one another; the sharp pavement cut
of shoes, piercing the night—the silence
of a basketball leaving the palm—
Better make it a good prayer.

ACKNOWLEDGMENTS

Portions of the first part of this manuscript were awarded The J. Kerker Quinn Award for Distinction in Creative Writing by the Department of English, University of Illinois in Champaign-Urbana (1995). "Circles" was included in the Asian American Artists Collective of Illinois (Spring 1993). "Dust" was awarded the Lowell-Grabill Creative Writing Prize at Wheaton College, Illinois (1996). "Song of Our Songs" was awarded the Faricy Prize for Poetry, Honorable Mention, at the Department of English, Northwestern University (Spring 2000). An Illinois Arts Council Fellowship was awarded in Summer of 2002.

Publication of other portions of the manuscript, "Night Sessions," are as follows, in chronological order: "Night Eyes," Mediphors: Literary Journal of the Health Professionals (Fall 1999); "Rain," Mississippi State University, Jabberwock Review (Summer 2000); "My Early Linguistic Lesson," University of Alaska-Fairbanks' Permafrost (Spring 2000); and "Grandmother's Watch" in the Saint Ann's Review of Saint Ann's College, NY (Fall/Winter 2000-1).

"Dust," in Missouri Western State College's The Mochila Review (Spring 2001); "Father" and "What is Still," in Princeton University's Theology Today (Spring 2001); "Learning to Read" in

Spalding University's (KY) The Louisville Review (Winter 200, Summer 2001); "Simplicity" and "Water Returning Back" in Glendale College's (CA) Eclipse (Spring 2001); "The Black Bear" in University of Alaska-Fairbanks' Permafrost (Summer 2001); and "Indian Summer" in the University of Texas-Pan American's RiverSedge (Fall 2001).

"Friend," "The Hyphen," "Night Sessions," and "What My Mother Says...," as well as "Song of Our Songs," and "After the Concert" and "The Ballerina," were published, along with a personal interview, in a chapbook-length series of poems in Illinois State University's The Spoon River Poetry Review (Winter 2001), as the "Illinois Featured Poet" of 2001. The poems were awarded the Illinois Arts Council Fellowship (Summer, 2002), mentioned previously.

"The Shaman," "My Bones," and "Driving Home" were published in Iowa State University's Flyway Literary Review, Asian American Special Issue (Spring 2002); "The Notebook" and "Wedding Pictures," in the University of Nebraska-Lincoln's Prairie Schooner (Summer 2002).

"Work," from the "Poems for Harry" section of this manuscript, were published in Many Mountains Moving (13th edition, 2002), special edition on "Literature of Spirituality," guest editor, Cathy Capozzoli. Poems and entire edited selection of creative works were nominated for the Utne Reader Alternative Press Award, Best Spiritual Writing (2002), ed. Philip Zaleski, and the Best American Poetry Series (2002), ed. David Lehman

The "Night Sessions" manuscript was semi-finalist for the Nicholas Roerich Poetry Prize at Story Line Press (2001), and Ashland Poetry Press's Richard Snyder Publication Prize (2001), and a finalist at Ohio State University Press's The Journal annual poetry prize (2002). Poems from this manuscript were published as a chapbook, Song of our Songs, by Finishing Line Press (July, 2010).

Other Books in the New Voices Series

A Day This Lit, Howard Levey

Kazimierz Square, Karen Chase

So Close, Peggy Penn

Silk Elegy, Sandra Gash

Palace of Ashes, Sherry Fairchok

Life with Sam, Elizabeth Hutner

GlOrious, Joan Cusack Handler

Rattle, Eloise Bruce

Soft Box, Celia Brand

Momentum, Catherine Doty

Imperfect Lover, Georgianna Orsini

Eye Level, 50 Histories, Christopher Matthews

Body of Diminishing Motion, Joan Seliger Sidney

The Singers I Prefer, Christian Barter

The Fork Without Hunger, Laurie Lamon

To the Marrow, Robert Seder

The Disheveled Bed, Andrea Carter Brown

The Silence of Men, Richard Jeffrey Newman

Against Which, Ross Gay

Through a Gate of Trees, Susan Jackson

Imago, Joseph O. Legaspi

We Aren't Who We Are and this world isn't either, Christine Korfhage

Elegy for the Floater, Teresa Carson

The Second Night of the Spirit, Bhisham Bherwani

Underlife, January Gill O'Neil